These Are My Shoes

Poems
by
Peter Money

Boz Publishing
163 Third Avenue, Suite 127
New York, NY 10003

Grateful acknowledgement is given to the following magazines and their editors for printing some of the poems that appear:

"Piazza Navona" in BALL PEEN; "Turnings" in BIG HAMMER; "Behind Me I Can Hear Them Talking" in BIG SCREAM; "Sitting Here Thinking About the Nature of Chaos", "The Hearts of Bees", "Three Settings" and "Freedom" in the CHIRON REVIEW; "Love" in the HAIGHT ASHBURY LITERARY JOURNAL; "To the Lady in Pink Standing Atop the Bridge" in LACTUCA; "Along FDR Drive", "In A Room", "6", and "The Ideal Statue Is The Living" in LAME DUCK; "Perennial" in NAPALM HEALTH SPA; and "One Man, One Country, One Language" in WE.

Thanks also to thank David Cope & Dave Roskos for their encouragement, THE PARIS REVIEW, and The Cummington Community of the Arts where some of this work was done.

This book is printed on recycled paper.

For my Parents,
For Lucinda.

vita brevis.

CONTENTS

ONE

TWO

THREE

FOUR

FIVE

SIX

SEVEN

This is life, still!
                     —Rimbaud

Out of the cradle endlessly rocking
                    —Walt Whitman

And you let them know why
                    —Abbie Hoffman

ONE

Turnings

Outside the turning of waves
in the Indian Ocean
tell me how I've come so far
and why and where and who I am
to be lying still in bed
under a fan and with the heat
I've locked myself in an 8 by 8
with basket walls and thatched floor
through the holes I hear different sounds
from tongues I'll never understand
I'm curled to pass some hours
creator show me what to do
how to venture along this beach
by myself not knowing to speak
to strange tides and stranger hands

the glow of a smoke on a bus
while a weird high-pitched woman
makes music squealing my head
I try to recline, shut my eyes
smell the residue of a native brand
the bus stops, we hear gypsies play
and all men take a leak on the side
the land of Cambodian schemes
of dry dust villages dark
shanties of stick and paper walls
past congregations worshiping fire
temples I've never seen before
Indians in lighted frames

'til here I am reciting words
inside this basket shell
I've so long to reach my home
and love the ones who are
safe away from dirty feet

from a world so much abused
who all use coinage the worth of tin
who eat their spicy foods
alone here is nearer to hell
save eyes and human hearts
who live in poverty

Freedom

Route 18 through Medina
the road, yellow passing in
her mirrored eyes (sunglasses)
obscured as in a dream, the road
a fisheye lens, maybe stoned,
yards passing, rolling by, Ohio.

Sheik Wild Cats from Detroit, strange
to see a black gang eating at the Inn
in Wellington, the "Lucky Few", black
leather riding jackets & Harley
Davidsons. Good to see the unusual.
Like Malcolm Forbes—he could be a moto-ganger too!
This is surely equality on
the streets of our nation's towns, yet
foreigners say "racists, sexists, capitalists".

We spend
the rest of the day
swinging in Findlay State Park
with the kids, the fat little girl,
remembering how we were scared
of heights—& wet buttocks on the slide
made squeaks like nails on a chalk board.
But when we were kids we didn't care.

On the rocks by the man-made lake
her eyes had many lakes, we
loved the day, the things we saw.
Returning, the road lines skated away
toward a horizon I'd return to &
it's the freedom to choose—

Sitting Here Thinking About The
Nature Of Chaos

did Nietzsche really
say "you need chaos
to make the stars dance?"
no, he said something
similar. I think that
Nietzsche could be wrong,
maybe the stars dance be-
cause they cannot be still.

wouldn't that be scientific,
to discover that stars dance

to give starbirths?

"chaos" is the name we give
misunderstanding

*

I've sat by this window
for most of an afternoon,
slept in front of it at night
& morning woke chilled.

the warmth is in the earth,
above it raindrops drape
the telephone line from the road
to the house, all day they don't fall.

*

water in the brook churning is
the washing machine between my

ears, the ferns along the drive
are prehistoric & have spines,
the birds think we're harmless,
everyone's inside today.

*

the stars are making children
somewhere over the mountain.

First Speech On Rain Forests & Cattle

What is the cost of the American Dream?
I will tell you, I understand
fast food joints get their meat from the south
americas, such as Argentina, and all those
rain forests are being chopped down to make
room for the cattle to graze or butchered
because outside America the talk is CHEAP
& inside America sometimes it's cheap too,
what they do to you that is, or even
what you do to yourself. I understand
I can't eat at fast food joints anymore
& that's going to be hard because I was raised
a suburban kid & going to McDonalds was always
a treat (though McDonalds came out publicly
& said they get their beef from other places,
that it's the other fast food joints who are
guilty of contributing to the chopping down of
rain forests).

       I guess I'm feeling guilty because
even though I was a vegetarian for two months
& even while I consider myself to be liberal-
hearted and wise enough to know better than to
wreck the world—
       I was raised a suburban kid and
it's going to be hard. I'm on the board of directors
for WHAT WE BREATHE. We all are. My skin's red,
white, & blue.

Soliloquy In April

If I were old enough to know what Woodstock Nation is
maybe I wouldn't face a blank white page, nor read
TIME which is really PEOPLE which is really TRUMP
which is really a different idea of DEMOCRACY which is
really DECLINE. Nor would I listen to Bob Dylan many years
too late singing "all I really wanna do°°°°°°°°oo" & I don't do
except to refrain, always refrain, from doing what's
productive: doing the laundry, grading 28 2.5 page essays,
making the bed, washing the dishes, it took me several
hours before I'd showered—what's going on? I should go
& buy a cup of cappucino, let it be my lithium, react
to the most dichotomous thermo-atom I know: me.

The wind blows the open yellow flower by the walkway
& all the green arms (spiked, rounded, stiff, loose)
bounce around & you can't tell me that they don't toil
too, they're a tide of strokes, soundless participators
in April.

TWO

Along FDR Drive

FDR's a black river snake
I feel comfortable riding
its shiny black-top home,
it takes me along glistening water
& lights make it something luxurious;
night making it calm on FDR seems to mum
this city
    bedsheets pulled to the noses leave
    only pairs of eyes
                alone expose in cold
                night—they become
                the sets of lights: sparkle, speak,

Seek
  inside New York
traffic moves so slowly with the luck of lights:
limousine lizards hog whole blocks on 2nd avenue:
waiting, sleeping, selling, who-knows?

Along FDR there's no sign of life—only speeds, bridges,
and the announcement of roads & advice of what not to do.

                      Where do the deer cross?
They do not. There are no deer here, there is
no Deer X-ing; one has not just left Albany driving
into the Berkshires, no, that kind of life is further north,
wilder, and maybe afraid of coming out.We should not be so
fortunate to be judged by our benevolent signs, one day
Martians or futurist historians will land & huddle around
our signs like "Deer X-ing" and think that they have found
a truly perfect world. Tell me they're not
                    so virtuous.
Blue-green bulbs—not sea or mountain themselves, but forming
the arcs of two mountains, or crests, a longhand letter "M"
strung to masts of the Brooklyn Bridge along FDR over the black
snake's shadow, shimmers silver-white oars of reflected light:

                              the eyes of somewhere, long
                              narrow like a serpent's, eyes
                              of water & air own this city
                              at night.
                                        For me, an invitation:
the bridge—not to jump but to walk; maybe tonight I'll tight-
rope walk, examining my footing over curiously
placed lamps—me,
atop an oriental gala, mountain, sea, illumination night!

                              We shall find out
                              many things...

We shall find out many things, tonight,
as it ought to be, a pleasurable drive.

To The Lady In Pink
Standing On Top The Bridge

O lady O lady the lights
behind me say hurry
say madness, emergency

the three lanes to Brooklyn
each jammed with drivers
& cops & an ambulance surge
onward, up the ramp
   on cathedral gates
you stand high
   in triforium
an opera of red
   lights beneath, loudly
the police intercom
   in traffic
      "PEOPLE MOVE TO YOUR LEFT
      OR TO YOUR RIGHT NOW!"
  & the white lights
   from their blue truck
      search for space to move,
  a rescue, headlights deaden
   my cabby's chinese face as he turns
     toward me, enigmatic,
       & so the cop—back on the PA
       shouts
        "CABBY USE YOUR BRAINS
         NOW MOVE!"
& we must all be fools on this bridge tonight
O lady
   O lady
     the lights
    sent to get you—pink,
      standing, will you
       dive while
       the cops

                    follow, their eyes
                  upon your figure,
                       do you use
                  the opportunity
                     as your church
                  do you wish
                  the scene gone?
                  SHOUT
"I've found my God, now go, leave me 'lone"
                  all the fuss
                    for your
                     standing—

the dispatcher
 over the cab
      radio announces "all cars stay clear
      the Brooklyn Bridge, they got a jumper"
                  & to the cabby I say
                  "did it look like she
                  was going to jump?"

we roll down the ramp to Brooklyn
   & my cabby says "Maybe. Maybe in the river—"
      his eyes are mostly white, so wide,
I turn to watch a pin drop,
   see it leap to nightsky
but Manhattan's yellow nightglow doesn't catch
   her
               & immediately after feeling
                  that close to the jumper,
                  I'm stunned,
                    no longer excited
                     by passing death, courage,
                  if only in a car
                maybe her life is saved. Or
                     maybe the cops look down,
                  no longer coaxing the dead
                       to live.
O lady O lady the lights
behind me say hurry
say madness, emergency

NYC Sanitation Workers

The garbagemen
               are cyclones
          moving in arcs
            scuffing clod feet
        between the back of their city truck
& yards
       twisting
            bending
hauling
     & heaving
             metal cans &
                       rubber pails
        into the mouth of a trash bin
                in wheels
                flinging empty containers
                aside
                like frisbees
                lids, cans,
                dead on their bellies
          a paper turns
           like ghost town brush
             dancing
           in arcs
           while
      a pizza box top
             flattens
                  petunias

                in our yard.

We Thieves

The brown sky, yes *brown*, rust ozone
top covers the north of Central Park
above still brown trees a brown derby
over Harlem, flat pan plane—derby sliced
like a brown wood frame, like a covered bridge
no bridge George Washington in this sludge,
battery acid empty doors old pictures dead
skin smushed prunes skid thick dirt road where
black & tan dogs chase & steal bones of chicken
into garbage streets & garbage cans & fire houses
black like a widow black like the sky over a toxic
island charred by stardom, but what human child
dreams of astronauts at the bottom of a murky pond?

  Pyres of burn
 ing grease
    cut &
 "poof" —the
slick is our sk
   y
     to
  day
an oil
     field tap
    estry
   no
   one
   can
   fly
  not
   even
    ali
    baba

-brown canvas
   prairie
dark
   pen dip
    ped
in wa
  ter
blee
  ding
    to the top;
   the liv
   ing wipe the
     ir
fe
et before ent
     ering
  the
  de
  ep
  e
  a
  r
  t
  h

THREE

My Country

There's an ocean in the country
listen, the trees are flagships
for more waves than Pan
could count
rain
light as mist & narrow
as latitudes of sand
touch the brooks—
rivulets begin at the sinking
drop, the imprint
two lovers accommodating
the new gift

there's traffic out of sight
diesel rrrmms
the tanker aground & the car
ferry positioning
for its docking, forward/
reverse, bow/
stern
the impatience
the passengers
harbor
the cumbersome
distractions
forget the sea
which
    be-got them
there—
someone tosses
the end
a cigarette
in the ever-
green camou-
flaged colored water

—gone under
           knocks
                 lifeless
           against the bulkhead

But that is far away in a cluttered bay,
inland
amongst people.

                 Here
           a mountain
            sends me idioms
           of sea
               washing
                     fresh
           see, far
               from towns & cities
           Here———
                        water teeming
           the smell of earth———

               &
                 at midnight the constellations
                 each shine
                    a sheep
                 pastures
                              buoy
                 in the cosmos
                         light as
                 diamond glazed
                 placenta
                    in the wake
                    of a divine trawler

the window curtain smooths my hand, white
the wind
blowing the configuration   of oceans
      through this country
        ready for sleep
           &
           wonder.

Sifting Through A Window

the green that lives
outside, makes phrases with wind—

a screen keeps us apart;

small birds "chirp"
unknowingly,

& these eyes fall to cheek bones.

"The spirit's not lost in broken bones"
I tell myself that
but these days I want to sit around and
draw circles over and over
and over like Yoshihara
when everyone else is making life-sustaining
decisions.

A Response

(for Amiri Baraka)

The opening of Toni Morrison's *The Bluest
Eye* is so abrasive I can't read it.
It's like looking into barbed wire (I have
a phobia—my eyes ache in front of sharp
objects)
      "   seeJaneseedickseeyoureyesbugOUT   "
& unjustified right hand margins
have   me
  read ing   so er
ratically   I
think I'll go
      crazy.
Then again it's
not too different
from poetry
     is it?
What's the big deal?
Maybe it's the way I am   today.
 May
   be
too much snot in my nose
       stops the mind
        anxiety's clogged
        impatience that's got to be
blown
  If I were
a painter   would I be
less anxious
  would days
  drift by in colors
  would turpentine impair
  my normal sense
  of reality
  would I be stoned
  would being stoned
  save me—

                    in grass fields
                              clouds
                    yellow suns,
                              beaches?
I'm still shaken-up about being
   the only white kid
     at a Marxists's jam session
   in Newark
     the old man's house
Professor
              his jazz
        is Pi-zazz
        raising Malcolm's ghost on MLK day
in a basement off Clinton street
        "You bother me I bother you back"
AveLou/ Ahbeyloo/ well Ave Maria
        I'm a people too
                    & I'm stroking my beard
        I don't like
                what I hear
   you'd kill me   if you could
    in those words
   you'd kill me   & yes
                    you had   in a poem
                                   & in your tone
                                something about...

    this *skin*.
                         "The pee-poll
                         U-nited"
            SLAM!
        UNITED?
   is that really what you
                    mean
                    on MLK
                         day?
            No, no, I see
               an Urban clan
                 propaganda say
                    come hear the jazz
                              band
                              play.

                                                   25

                                        Heck.
                                        I thought
                                        I was going to a nightclub
                        even put on
                        a white shirt,
                        tie, & button dn.
                        sweater. wool
                                   slacks, dress
                                   shoes polished
                                   no clothes to fight
                                   a revolution in.
Could be
  I'll listen
to Country Music
   drive black Victoria (50s
pickup truck) wear boots
                           in summer
                     chew straw
                     throw stones
                                   burn leeches off
                                       my skin
                        w/ a Lucky Strike
                           keep roads dusty
                           & in winter
                           spread with snow.
Call me provincial
              now
           call me
            a sore loser
           call me satisfied
           call me
                 taken aback
                 by modern times
Look, I know all about it:

           The chinese graves all washed away
           —buried *them* too close to the river;

imagine diggers
 panning for gold
   scooping their railroad
from tin plates

              & bones floating down the river
                                they were
              gone,
                        same as old Tobe's marker,
                        the adopted Indian
                        arrowheads taken
                                grazed over by other
                                family names
"Cuts yr hair frm Tobes"
        in his cottage barbershop
          business in the livingroom
          & I guess
            the wife slept
            in the back.
        Did Tobe have a wife?
        Tobe had a marker,
        a stone, once.

In Napa Valley—"Prunes to be picked, boy!"
  a dollar & more a day, boy! call it
    depression, call it immaterial what was
            in yr pocket,
            it was
            good
        as barn raisin'
            good
        as a home cooked meal
        brought behind the house
    to feed the Mexican family
            good as a church supper, hell!

Communism wasn't called bad names then
            communism was all of those things I mentioned,
it was down-right democracy only
    democ-
    racy didn't know it then.

The depression musta brought it
or the wagon train or some
ideal called America on a frontier—
            on an escape from persecution
            (a royally sponsored renascence—)

　　　　　　hard seas Melville never saw
　　　& birthing Dr. Williams never felt
　　　　　　　　but in the palm of his hand
　　　about a woman & in a poem
　　　　　　　　　the gritty roads & dusty daughters
　　　　　　　　might've loved
　　　　　a few natives—
　　　　　　—in time.

I can't write like Welton Smith
　　　　about Malcolm
　　　　　　or *da da da* like LeRoi *his*
　　　　business card
　　　　　　　　　　syn-
　　　　　　　　　co-
　　　　　　　　　　　　pates
　　　　　　　　　through cribs
　　　　　　　　　in the ghetto
　　　& on land
　　　like the earliest
　　　　　sounds
　　　　　he call
　　　A F R I C A
—no aborigine name
　　　A F R I C A
—no apparition
　　　A F R I C A
　　　　　　　the primal
　　　　　　　spirit
　　　　　　　　beats &
　　　　　　　taps
　　　　　　& yells
　　　　　& gets down
　　　　　　to bodies
　　　　　　moving
　　　　　　alive.
　　　　　　That's it.

Proclaim　　Proclaim　　Proclaim
　you own the world when you
　　　　　write!

28

You raise peoples from the dead
    & swept away, you branch
            stories
have no place in people's lives
    unless they
                want to
                step back
                        tap tap
                & hear it
                        tap tap
                hear what's going
                on
                tap tap
        Ahbeyloo Ahbeyloo
            Ahbeyloo Ahbeyloo
        Ahbeyloo Ahbeyloo
—this is what they call
                me
                    in basements in
                        Newark
                    on a Broadway stage
                        in
                    South Africa
                        RESPOND
                        RESPOND
    call me that & I'll sit quiet.
    your grief is a screened door to me
                    circa 1963.

Where does a slander come from?

Ahbeyloo,
        Ahbeyloo, "jims"
jack/john/dick/sam/sally/joe—
        "jims" were not
        my fathers. "jims"
        were not my mothers.
        Mine were, o.k.,

Johns
   & Helens
      & Elizabeth
    —anglo names
    but
    movers &
    farmers &
not
    Ahbeyloo, Duma,
we never knew that name.
         we are
         here,
         we are
         here,
         RESPOND
         RESPOND
    this is my
    call
    we are here
    beside
    we are here
    to hear the calling
    not dampen the
    tap tap
    of your foot,
    your stone, Welton,

    but to marvel
    as you do.

    we are here.

FOUR

The Evergreen Review, 1968

The Incredible string Band's hippie faces
hats & scarfs & kids right there with the adults
all in the groove for the album photograph
an ad for "The Hangman's Beautiful Daughter"
songs "guaranteed to pull   you out of any blues
and into the fun of   walking down the
streets of an old   part of town" by Terry Bér
a book called *Sexual Adventure In Marriage* —"ten-
day free examination copy"   50 selections from
the Soviet Army Chorus & Band including that favorite
"Volga Boatman" and also "Volga Bargehaulers" and
not to forget "From The Volga To The Don."
                    Not satisfied?
Bagpipes & Drums—STEREO—or, Country Joe & the Fish
are you-
            "The things that you are:
                questioning, idealistic,
                    concerned
                    with the love, the confusion
                    and the excitement of the life
                    you live today; this is
Country Joe & the Fish are you, on Vanguard
95c for a paperback   Fidel Castro's hands on
Che Guevara's Bolivian war diary   then Minister
of Information of the Black Panthers Eldridge Cleaver
wanted to be a lawyer, started cutting marijuana
to get through school   beat up Hunkies—paddy hunting
on the weekend Gut Theatre in the streets of Spanish
Harlem 'cause "They don't need *Hamlet*" as Jones
told Papp   & for the auto lover "The saga of
Mercedes..." —the pointed helmets & the man
behind the machine   projecting a model for manhood
in *Evergreen*! The Age of Revolution fresh from Grove
Kensington Market rock-men from Canada recorded
in Manhattan—prestigious sessions—The Fugs, I can
hear them saying in 1988 at the Bottom Line
"it crawled into my hand, honest" dayglo pyre
for $1.98 "Suppose They Gave A War And Nobody Came"

Janis Ian, The Mecki Mark Men, The Split Level, Joan
Baez & Baptism The Adventures of Phoebe Zeit-Geist
from a) Molested by a giant lizard! to z) Assaulted
by Zeppelins! She does *not* hostess Tupperware parties
get gift subscriptions to *Family Circle* belong to
Weight-Watchers collect green stamps/ plaid stamps
to obtain a free electric rotisserie nor watch
"The Dating Game" Serendipity Singers, Morning Glory
a conversation with Abu Amar "the Muslim Che
Guevara"—bringing peace to Arabs and Israel—WOW!
        They were on top of it man!
Timothy Leary's "the Magical Mystery Trip"
pricks & mothers a poem about penislore by *FIEL*ds
GM's '68 Camero whipping around hairpins
above St. Tropez (BIG V8) *The Sex Game*
of Prentice-Hall "promises no miracles of adjust-
ment" songs of Leonard Cohen ("Hey, That's no way
To Say Goodbye"—"Suzanne") At last:
Soviet Master Agent Kim Philby & as always,
Strange Posters Radio City Station
New York, New York WOW!
What've we been doin?

Among Whales

As you know

       we should make use of this time

we are dying.

The repetition of our breaths

will declare; we are the most supple now,

our lives may weaken   as the natural world

deepens its embrace

we take turns—

keeping time—

three faithfuls

cut

and counting,

rising to forbid our cold grave

from closing;

Measure us.   Measure our time.

He's The Boy

He starts out about his life
in the starched-dry cornfield town
making pianos sound better

& of course enter a girl,
now a woman, & several months
of screwin' around & occasionally
drinking at a local tap

& in public places lightin' up
those Eastwood filterless tar candies
& blowing breathless into the air
of empty little town, dirty little
life on the make without a car

& nowheres to go anyway. Enter a girl
another woman—& seeing the old ones
is hard too, 'cause the feelin's still
there behind the blue eye, beneath the pack
of Chesterfields in the chest pocket

the dry throat thirsty—
screwing kindly like a job he's good at,

there's this need to move on

Men

Many pretty young women ride the train
from the north, some with their boyfriends
& some sleeping, curled, or— the outstretched
leg tracing the long line of the letter "Z",
their knees pulled to their own breasts, making
babies in their sleep, by themselves, their knapsacks
on the empty seat next to them.

I glance out of habit   as I glance
out the window, moving, at New England
homes along the inlets—how it looks like Maine
& I'm as far south as New London! (Not south
for some)
     Beautiful things

& by nature
I'm wanting my partner
to return, and every woman
reminds me of her, who reminds me of her
if only for her sex: they are alike,
insofar as I desire to look
—and then to stare long
to the waterways & the two lovers
walking on the rocks that cobble
the shore, bending for a shell
—I don't know for sure, too far
for me to really see—I'll bet
their hands are cold, but alive in the way they res-
pond to each other's stiff fingers   the moment
before entrance and sprawl,
that long journey back to New
York.

Many of the young women happen
to have well cared for blond hair—silk

& satin—perty noses & narrow svelte lips
to slow dance when they smile.

Their sweaters and shirts are loose to fashion
& their jeans are not, as well. Their shoes slip off,
they have no strings, their toes are cupped in cotton.

I would be "better" if I kept this to myself,
but I want you to sense the desire a stranger can feel:
we open our hearts to the Great
                Wall of China
        we open our hearts to Sphinx & wraiths
                like Cleopatra
        we open our hearts to the Bay of Fundy
                & falling stars
        we open our hearts to evergreen boughs
                in our dreams,
how shallow waters become deep
when the relative size is a hermit crab—that's the key.
*

A bottle in one hand
the other around her
neck
a song in drunken stupor
her hands by her side
it's the Sunday night routine,
maybe every night, it's Mall Babies
of a different mall, it's old men
& woman in love with night while
the booze lasts they're getting
very old partying underground in Manhattan

it's men & woman outside the Bowery
Bank beneath Madison Square Garden,
—like teenagers lining the wall of a gym
after a rough dance, one guy laid-
out in the boys' bathroom
a belly to the light in the ceiling
his mother'll be mad, no,
his mother's out with the out-of-work
whiskey salesman, pork-n-poetry,
kids on a Sunday night
they know better but it isn't worth the fight,
not even on Easter, drink up!

*

Kennebunkport: hold those yachts straight
while God brushes his teeth in the side
of a slice of fiberglass—
get yourself ready for our Maine man: Mr. President!

And yet I have a confession: I've looked at yachts
from both sides now
& still, somehow,
it's life's illusions I recall...

*

2 young people—
maybe in love—
turn the pages
of the program
from the New York
Auto Show, & con-
jure, maybe, the
cars between them.
His arm's around
her neck.

a man asks for money,
he offers a paper cup,
the 2 young people
study the automobiles
even closer &
when he passes
the young man looks up,
narrows his eyes
on the poor man's back,
then goes back to viewing
the expensive wheels
                    & I think I've been both of them, once.

*

Men say,
        "just gimme something I can call 'my baby'"

The Moon

Last night driving the moon
hung low in the early morning sky
a dull orange bowl, half a cantaloupe,
half a skull yellowed by age
the moon began to fall

Perennial

Do not rain, Tomorrow,
For I am thin
And Growing takes such strength
And sorrow.

The Ideal Statue Is The Living

Talk to me of sweet silences
how Apollo arches his legs
aiming his arms towards Heaven
how he defies gravity there
on a bronze pole for his balance.

Days my friend spun in the kitchen!
In our thin apartment, ballet
we called the dance "the kitchen spin"
even one night when a car sped
into his back, he spun away!

Talk to me of sweet silences
of statues cast immortal,
of victims the statue's ideal;
Apollo can aim for Heaven
but my friend is already there.

Talk Talk Talk Talk Talk Talk Talk Talk
Silences Silences Silence
meter the meter the meter
is dead dead dead dead dead is dead
but spun into tragedy, spins—

Concerning Artifact:

We are the exceptions.
Those who listen to soundless
reverberations of a keyboard
because it's in the empty space
we start to understand
the language of gesture, or
greater still, of thought.

We are the outcasts
in a region of flash & fireworks,
we shun the raunchy repertoire
of those who take for granted,
of the miser who's forgotten he ever had
neighbors.

We are the frustrated
when all around bodies covered with
glitter flaunt & extol
the deprivation of another.
How is it those familiar lyrics
have various meaning?
            What so proudly
              we hailed

   It is a fair thing
We live by the grave,
counting blessings,
counting mounds of earth and
reasoning with stars, counseling with ocean.
It's a fine thing we can see our reflection
in granite.

6

O, my head I wanna sleep
   you look so sleepy, too, placid, white, warm
   pillow over your head you've had since
   you were a baby. We seem so dead
   when we're asleep, I imagine me
   as you are, exhausted, bereaved,
   left to figure it all out in rest
   I never remember. You, though, dream
   nightly and tell me of a life
   I'm jealous of, although scared of,
   because the places I could go
   might repeat themselves in the passing
   of a car or a person or in a certain
   kind of rain, velocity and sound.
O, my head I wanna sleep
   the day has begun too soon, dark,
   we move like snowdrifts when we're asleep.

FIVE

Reckoning

a generation of radical poets are our professors
  now; the academies await their criticism
  while the kids fall in love with their words
  their own —the same
  old politics, have we become that lost? Invention,
  have the chemicals of Johnson & Dow eaten you?
  (Websters hasn't changed that much)
What's left to do? Is Whitman too old to turn to?
Is Ginsberg too young? Too willing Bodhisattva?
  As man
   as teacher
          as savior
                is still
                    a man

& all the world inspires me as does a man
  as does a woman   which comes first?

I'm wanting so
to follow footsteps
following in my own pattern
not stopping to begin anything new & know about it
but to begin without knowing
                        but
too late to be carried through Prague as May King,
instead I must watch flowers
                        & balloons in Moscow,
from ABC images of a kinder, gentler, Marx, Stalin,
   & Lenin.
& What *if* Malcolm & MLK had arm wrestled?

*

Where're the radical ideas of invention?
  Where's the Jackson Pollock? Where's his mother?

We must search
around the normal
sources, & guess

making new
   forms from history (that great future!)
with our burnt & still trusting hands
   saving what worked well
& savoring why what didn't

How does electricity bend? Our kind have found
   in a dream we'll conjure the representation
   of our given realities, we'll call it music
         it is
               & uses that foul
         clanging of manmade objects
               a "found" poem!
         finds a melody, a lick,
a whale.
         R.E.M. is a band I listen to
   in the morning before I go to work
   & at odd hours to stimulate my blood
blood must move
& we must move
blood about souls
      Dream then. Ask yourself why
         Rimbaud stopped writing poems
      then use that answer to write more
         & "get plenty of sleep before
      the exam; take no stimulants; good—-

luck", I won't say byebye
      I won't giveup   coffee
      until coffee uses me as its mess
      & says: look, this is a crack baby,
               he was born with this disease...you
   can't change him. only move with song
& sooth.

      *

48

       take it to sleep
the poem
    will be in New Orleans
        by afternoon

 rain's in the sky
softballs hail
    on the panhandle,
      tornados—
    the dancin' jazz
      at Will & Val's
    weddin', catfish
      on friday!

*

blood in the fishbowl,
    we need to take care of
        the fish we eat.

*

One Man, One Country,
One Language

Lots of people saw him and thought he was
the next Hemingway, the next Pound. He wrote furiously
in a tattered notebook he always kept close to him. His
clothes were ragged and his hair, by public standards,
was a nest. Lots of people saw him and thought he was
brilliant:

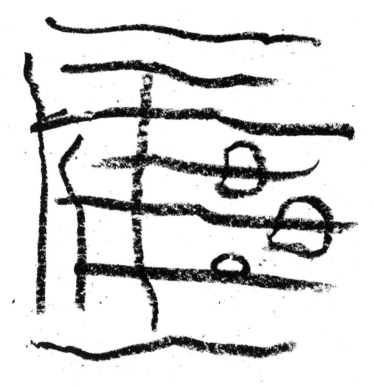

And he was.

Some Good Photos

There's a phrase he likes using now
he says it sums-up quite a bit of the way
things seem to be happening these months,

he's always ending sentences now with "etc.,etc.,etc."
Two and a half weeks in Antigua
trompin' sea grass,
white sand public access,
flora—palms, flame trees,
goats, chickens,
cows all over the place
fish you'd see in a tropical tank,
star fish wriggled around &
regular, Angel fish—
a sugar mill place;
people with an odd slow pace to 'em
and everyone who did things
was black. It was odd.

The government's making a hotel there
and they've got thirty rooms filled
while they finish with the other 200
—the government gets shares in any
new development.

Back in the states, etc. etc., he says
we're all splittin' up and goin'
our separate ways, etc. etc.
—that's about it. etc. etc. etc.

*

I said he'll have to show me
his shots of Antigua before he moves west.

I could hear him light-up over the phone.

51

Metronome

Walking west on 59th street
a blind woman taps
her pointer

along the sidewalk

walking east, a young man
going to work
listens

*

a heartbeat keeps them both
alive

Uncle's Greenhouse

Do you remember when
    we pulled Cokes from a slot
        how the orange was usually
        on the bottom—

For a quarter?

And there was a place on
    the right-hand side:
        the bottle opener
            caps fell down

    What a great action:

    chicfusss-tingk

    a kid's strength
    breaking the top
    of the soda pop

We'd always try to pull
each bottle
like checking for dimes
in payphones

On Loving An Ex

looking
for sparks

among
ashen coals

is like
returning

to the
arboretum

that now
harvests

condominiums

Teakettles, The Moon

Landed in Vermont, I find myself spreading ash
over the icy driveway on the plateau where the house
sits, something of an Alice Springs with trees all
around—tall, several dozen thick pine trees
 seem to brace the sky along the upward driveway
  & around the house at the ridge, the trees
        create a natural parthenon in the vein
        of Maxfield Parrish—& at night the snow lawn
        glimmers blue under the wide eye of the moon
          high above the chicken coop. Ash will help
          our footing.
                One pine, behind the coop, is the size
                of a silo. The chickens sleep near
                its stem.
                   I wonder,
                what do chickens look like
                when they're asleep—
                teakettles?

The moon's a mystery to me & that's no mystery at all,
as it's a mystery to most—perhaps even to those
who've walked its surfaces—jumped, bounced,
—I'm an acolyte & the moon's my catechism;
  I become fixed, blank, my cells freeze under hot
  ice, the moon's glow, is this demagoguery?

The golden dog wags his tail.

We're far from Islam & yet I've been
thinking about Islam for several days: how
the masses want to massacre the author of a western
book, a fiction.

The moon is not worth killing for, but I
would be sorry to see it go.

On Poetry and Paint

How do you paint

a still life

when
        painting's
                a waterfall?

SIX

The Hearts Of Bees

(for Medbh McGuckian)

Yours will be perfect
in Ballycastle dew
writing in the morning
an Irish poet
virgin hands
your girly stocking white face
the schoolgirl long skirt
poetry
moaned softly
red
for you

I listen to the blues
of flowers
so clear
took
the hearts of bees

You are not, girl, a performance suicide
you greeted as you sashayed

Yours will not be a 20 inch coffin, no woman:
in the middle
blue can go from black
& white
around the small island you made
& make the hard ice
the cheeks of you
with
the hair
spines, pages to ends,
flowers becoming
bees

61

No "only" voice, your cry
was met by flowers
and clenched them
blue
with a pen, you were greeted

Three Settings

1.
In our bedroom,
she reads to me a story:
10,000 butterflys were released
in the hall of a Chilean ball

& fluttering to fluorescent lights
fell dead within minutes

like the doves freed at games
who fly into the engines of planes—

2.
Almost noon on a Saturday in June,
the livingroom window open—street
level sounds; "Jessie" is called,
tags on Jessie's collar jingle.

We need no music in our apartment,
we listen from across the street
to country twangs—fiddle, banjo,
dirt roads, oak trees with carved
love initials,
        fables, broken-down
automobiles in the front yard left
for fixing; the porch on the square
wooden house smiling, a little, with
drunken lips, like the softened rubber
of a worn shoe, a curve in the middle.

3.

Only last night we were in
each other's cold arms, warming,
smelling the claret being sipped
by a middle aged european couple
on a blanket next to us.

                        Urban folk
submit to the open air opera,
chorus rising out of darkness,
stars from the city! Life forces,
whispers, between two huddled
closely & listening
—in Italian.

In a Room

So many crooked nights, the beetles search for an opening
in the room where windows are screened
We all search for livable space, isn't that what we really do?
And within white walls a typewriter key smacks erasable paper
because it is an attempt at explaining where the summer is going.
The Renoir girl in Juanita's painting knows of this pondering:
sorrowful introspection by a stream of garden,
flowers of green and gold and pink, orange they try to light
a dejected man's day. But the girl knows.
Debts still owed keep the body close to home;
a spirit yearns to escape, the flying creature trapped within walls.
The pilgrimage isn't that far away and it is
Will that shall carry the wanting to their destination.
Prayer is the thing that can't be reconciled with now
that days are back to getting shorter.
Letters left opened, scattered about a room still
unsettled need answering—but so does the poem,
incredible sky-dive, a realization of dying.
The first swim of the season awaits an awakening:
salt water will be swallowed in the throat,
bathers survive, some will open their eyes under water
feeling the sting and certain redness
the eye will look exhausted and ready for sleep.
Others may be raising a bottle in toast: "L'chayim!"
to us, for the moment,
while two people sit in separate cities reminiscing early morning
hours away with ill-satisfaction that life's a momentary thing,
for these moments seem eternities. For one
the cigarette softens the head—someone has just let the beetle free
and all anxiety is released in the soaring away from the light,
a bulb it was once attracted to.

I Watched Waves, Without You

I watched waves without you
and smiled when salt-spray
touched my lips, my cheeks,
nose, eyelids.

I watched waves without you,
strong, green marble cake,
this noon, sitting on wooden steps
recollecting kisses.

I watched waves without you,
pounding the bottom of stairs,
feeling triumph and defeat,
and shivering.

I watched waves without you,
the submission of white caps,
their roar turning to silent snow—

Chant

Sitting on a concrete slab
once a dock
Calungute Beach darkens
beautiful red sun,
biggest head,
to a pinpoint.

East Indian tourists
chat after dinner
on cooling sands.
Westerners are in their rooms.

Bells like an eastern dancer's
feet ring rhythmically
when the sugar cane gets squeezed
into a drink by the vendor.

I sing to myself,
vexed by apocalyptic movie
and nirvana,
chanting—

Ra na ah se yo o ka la ra ma ba
Ko ho ah a te ra ma—
te ra ma ha-ha se yo
oh o kam ne ah a se de o
la se ra ma he te ko o ta
ah te yo o ko dam na te
Deo bor ay ko in ah—a la ko se
En ah-a la lan for or yo me.

(India)   Why'd I pass that man
                 chained to a tree?

                      In Goa
                      Hot Goa
                      Brown turning
                      Sea

                 I bought Goldman's *The Color of Light*
                 and ditched Sam Hunt's poems

                      In Goa
                      Hot Goa
                      Brown turning
                      Sea

                 Ate prawn and fried rice
                 drank pints of Kingfisher beer

                      In Goa
                      Hot Goa
                      Brown turning
                      Sea

                 Chased by vicious dogs after midnight
                 after smoke from Nepal, heat lightning

                      In Goa
                      Hot Goa
                      Brown turning
                      Sea

                 The hot bus back to Bombay
                 In time for Easter

                 The driver praying along the way
                 At roadside altars
                           *

(Egypt)   Pyramids forgotten with a frown,

              Kept captive in a perfume shop.

              A robed man walking toward me

              From out of the desert

              Carrying a bottle of Pepsi.

Piazza Navona

I.

Cobble stones
open air cafes
water sounds
the 19 yr. old couple
kissing, leaning on
the 300 yr. old building.
Romantico Roma
restaurant refugees
street socials
politica poetica
panorama
stays with changes
changes and stays
new people occupying
an older condition.

II.

A purple balloon like a lengthy phallus
floats straight into the early evening
yellow-blue where birds like bats
swarm over rust colored stone flats
with balconies and red, pink, and violet flowers
green around their venetian slats
around the obelisk where huge Roman men
support a rock fountain, water flows
around an angry lion caught in gushes
and serpents lashing in a moat
all for happy people pausing in the still & moving
atmosphere of a square where artists with clean bibs
and hands are seen hawking prefab masterpieces;
a man plays jazz on a bamboo sax while fashion
kids wear sunglasses into dusk, and time really
hasn't stopped, no, preserved and going-
on, connected interchangeably with the past.

The Lawn Man Behind The Vatican

Of all the treasures
  Raphael's and Michelangelo's
  and Sistine Chapel men
  muscled and naked or
  with a pen, the book, so deep
In thought on palace, on papal walls

The little man in white cap
  like a painter's, blue shirt and pants
  and little brown boots
is the most wonderful
  how he pats the lawn with concise steps
  he paces Giant's feet and bends
  for a weed, the devil,
  he is in charge of four squares
  of lawn and fountains
  grooming & keeping lush
  plush his garden his palace his work-
  place clinking an iron rod on stone
  walks and turning his cane in
  a lock to open five dozen sprinklers
How he walks among statues!

Traveler In New Zealand

So many s^{t}a^{r}s

I can't believe it!

the face in the window

is m ^{i} n ^{e} !

SEVEN

Waking

Between louvers
spread with dust
vacant white metal
chairs balance in
the wind.

The long arms of
bushes nod.
The red hammock rocks
its red boat.

A hazel profile of
stairs leads to the deck
where the landlord retrieves
her laundry. At night it's
an observatory between brown
apartments.

Coffee percolates
along with Mozart
at 6:05 in the evening
& I wake.

Out back a beach ball
figure eights, over time,
in Sylvie's green sandbox
filled with water.

Liquid music runs
electric between my
sternum & adam's apple.

The blue star dances on the turtle.

Neighbors

I.   At camp
       a fire burns
           the belly of a round black stove,

       a gas light
       clearing a spot
       on a frosted window

       begins a weekend.

          Outside, the brook's
       frozen power:
             falls
               steps
     —robes & hands of marble,
       a memorial in moonlight.

II.   Old Frenchy gets by
       on no electricity year round,

       where the sheep live, he lives.

       & frankly, even if satellite dishes were
       affordable, they'd be much too cumbersome
       around the old cars & stumps

III.   The state stocks the brook
       with browns.
       Rainbows are indigenous.

       Any way you look at it, trout tastes good.

Whiteout

So this is how it must have been
before the age of electric light
when families gathered by the fireplace
reading quietly and sleeping while
outside starlight was being filtered
by dense particles of snow
milking the landscape outside the window
bowing the arms of fir trees reverently
blurring vision so that the house across the street
becomes a stark and marble monastery
where a solitary man is believed to be bundled
in heavy quilted blankets in a corner bed
who hears the sound of menacing limbs
scraping the house-side, irritating his sleep.

In the single footed path that in summer's a road
a single caller files with high steps
in drifted snow, a lantern carried waist high
firm by a chilled stiff hand
makes his way home after visiting a friend
and hot toddy with scone
one observes from a dark house
the sound of winds, footsteps,
and the whispers of snow like scurrying sand.

Resting In Vermont

Capture the snow
blue in the light
of the moon's glow
colors the summit
a navy spine
& the valleys
left in shadow
still the wind

the magic blows
away with sleep
& wakes me
frosted in wonder

Behind Trees

When they push and shove and shout slurs
am I scared? When I can't see their faces
wrapped in hats and scarfs—the only ones
on a dark street, am I scared? When their
shadows slip behind me as I'm walking to
the store and their voices quiet for then,
am I scared? Am I scared on my own street
at eight in the evening when no one's beside
me? I've got thirty-six dollars in my pocket,
a used leather coat, and floppy sneakers,
am I scared? Am I scared to live in the city?
Wasn't the woods scary once when practically
nothing would sound?

Behind Me I Can Hear Them Talking

Behind me
I can hear them
talking, he's complaining
to her he's saying
You can't even walk,
that there are too many
People, he says *I wish*
a disease would come and
wipe out half the people,
in a kind of bored &
monotone type of voice
& I look at him walking,
walking steadily
without stumbling
as though through a field—
side by side he & she
in synchronicity &
I call out to him as he's
moving ahead of me *Would you*
be one of them? But he doesn't
hear me or it doesn't matter,
he was moving just fine,
maybe a bad day, but I'm left
standing in front of
the Woolworth entrance
staring at him & wondering
what *Half* he thinks
he belongs to

Sometime Clicking

What was that of the process of the heart?

> "All of his life is dedicated to discovering
> how he fits into this great puzzle, this
> master plan, to God and his country."

The song brought tears to his eyes,
the photograph of waves.

> "From London we'll take a train to the
> SeaLink."

That sea would be crossed again,
a venture to collect

portfolios of people
dialects and reasoning,
tongues as frequent and individual
as waves cut by a ship.

And they were photographed,
the successive rolls of twenty-four
thought by a few to be wasted. Rather,
the experience was of clicking:

> in moments as spontaneous,
> curious as the heart.

> "When I travel, I try to be selective."

He remembers clicking and
how much he got wet.

Love

A couple embraces
against closed doors

I walk by
her eyes gleam
into a spot of her own.

Once home,
I lay my suit down
and rest on the bed.

Some Kind Of Party

My Dad's not an old man but I'm not a boy anymore either.
I had just had my morning coffee and told him I'd get my shoes
on and come up to help him. He was on the roof pulling trees
by their branches "otherwise moss will grow on the roof" he said.
I've been scared of heights for years and my Dad, who wants
to retire next year, is standing in his dungarees and white
T-shirt. He tells me to grab a branch and pull so he can saw
it off. As I pull I feel my rear end inching its way down the
slope of the roof so I say "Dad hurry if you can."

When it comes to getting down off the roof I say to my Dad
that maybe he ought to go first. "But do you need me to hold
the ladder for you?" My Dad doesn't need me to hold the ladder
for him. When it's my turn he tells me how close my foot is
to the top rung of the ladder and tells me to "be sure and put
all of your weight over the roof."

In the supermarket I'm the only one in line with a pint
of ice cream. Everyone else had foodstuffs and airfreshener.
The girl with braces on her teeth puts one of those plastic-
stick dividers between my pint of ice cream and her mother's
airfreshener.

My Dad's Toyota stationwagon can go fast when I floor it to take
a no-traffic opportunity by the hand when it comes. It's summer
and there are too many people.

I can't believe I said that: that there are too many people.

That was the kind of day it was.

There was a war brewing in the Persian Gulf
I feared
and a soldier of America's Stark returned
anxious to spend time on the beach and watching girls.
The newsman said he's nineteen.
Who am I to say where he belongs?

*

"They're just dead things" my Dad calls
the branches he cuts
(I'd warned him about his own
environmental morals)
"They're just dead things."

I'd forgotten about the manila folders
stuffed in the back of my closet, in my parents'
house,—hats, baseball cards, Matchbox cars from childhood,
boxes filled with letters of a first love and friend
already sealed themselves back together again
over summers in heat, locked words sealed their abscess
and without my doing shut their lips with secrets.

Not staying, moving helps me define who I am.
And things—things I've collected, I shall have a pile
on my grave, build a fireplace and tell stories!

*

Momentum offers to us
a chance to rest, the escalator,
lifting us to the ledge
where we cascade forward
to turnstiles and direction
to jobs and wandering
(but some always walk
up the moving stairs)
to the beat of a timer.
Could be they're fighting
a clock, punching exact
tattles from a wall.

A misfortune, even if one likes
the pace, to be so on time,
but understanding to one
who lives off meter and rhyme.

*

84

One, Murray, wanted to be a famous artist
and so hundreds of pages of drawing paper
and bone white canvases stretched and nailed to
wooden frames, supports, windows with permanent shades
wait and turn yellow, painting their own memoirs
because Murray is grown now and can only dream.

*

The crazy man walks
by with his news-
paper cupped in his hand
and folded like a bat,
a club raised to his head
simultaneous with his fist,
elbows pound the air, cries
in his black rain coat
nonsense to the passer-by.
This is the world, I think,
this is the world as I see it

and the people in the street are
my brothers, sisters, we'll not admit.

*

Twice a Priest has passed me by
my beacon or greeting unanswered
in fact unacknowledged
except in the sneer of their faces
later I accept
they are no holier than I

Service.
My friend waits on tables
where people tell him "fetch
more bread" and the first thing
comes to mind: BREAD FOR THE WORLD
Oh—the bread we order and never eat.

This kind of night
I like to sit, the windows open
for sounds and cool air, I get to wear
something heavy around my shoulders
looking from picture to picture and
trying to foresee when Bill will die
and take his Japanese flower
arrangements with him, the world will carry
on under its same madness and
perhaps Bill will miss how mad it always was.

I wonder if Jesus felt the hands of Lepers long after
saying goodbye and "have fun" like Bill did—
my right hand tingled all the way home.

I felt my face and it felt realer.

That night I couldn't sleep
branches were falling
with particles of retrospection
seeing the most beautiful
and wonderful instances
lived on, each, really as a dare
that heart-line, that string.

The walls came alive that night
well, not the walls but the pictures
in my bed, a body sleeping
next to me where I sat stiff
with eyes cut narrow then widening
to absorb the impressions
made on brick, the paintings
in the black room balancing

their gray dimensions above
the bookcase against the wall

in a ghostly residue
like filtered smoke, hospital gauze,
the essence, maybe, of them

appearing at dreaming time
less the picture, more the sense
of entities you must reach
to see, the puzzlement of
veiled reality, in night time
dream of waking gifts.

I witnessed the saints' wish on me.

A voice saying "speak ye your Mantra,
remember the sky, the wind curving backs
of green grass blades on the cliff's
edge, above 700 feet of roaring ocean
air, remember these above all."
My temple throbs, a coming stroke?
I must tame myself, tame, before
the desecration of all good
within me combats the pressure
of deadlines unsuccessfully.
But this becomes my religion
when the gathering of people
mauls the willingness to concede
my individuality to my God.

& if the touch of people were not
so real
my hands might grow
'narley & my trunk might cave in,
like father before me, the expected surprise.
Friends, family—watch the new portraits dry:
this's our lifetime, seen among the centuries
painted, printed, played the contemplative tune
then gone—like some kind of party that's talked about
& then forgotten, trashed with the minutes
for only tomorrow, for tomorrow we live on.

My prayers stream out like expectation.

This is Peter Money's first book of poetry.
He was born in California, lived in Vermont,
and grew up on Cape Cod. He is a graduate of
Oberlin College, he has worked many odd jobs,
and he has traveled around the world. He has
recently studied with Allen Ginsberg, Susan
Fromberg Schaeffer, and Joan Larkin at
Brooklyn College where he presently teaches
English Composition. He lives in Brooklyn,
New York.